M000080617

FAIR
GAME

FAIR GAME

A Lady's Guide to Shooting Etiquette

by Piffa Schroder
with illustrations by Timothy Jaques

Ashford Press Publishing
Southampton
1988

Published by
Ashford Press Publishing 1988
1 Church Road
Shedfield
Hampshire SO3 2HW

British Library Cataloguing in Publication Data

Schroder, Piffa
  Fair game.
  1. Great Britain. Game animals. Shooting
  I. Title   II. Jacques, Timothy
  799.2′13′0941
  ISBN 1 85253 190 8

Printed by Hartnolls Limited,
Bodmin, Cornwall, England

To my daughter,
Leonie

CONTENTS

A FATHER'S ADVICE TO HIS SON

If a sportsman true you'd be
listen carefully to me:
never never let your gun
pointed be at anyone;
that it may unloaded be
matters not the least to me.
When a hedge or fence you cross
though of time it cause a loss,
from your gun the cartridge take
for the greater safety's sake.
If twixt you and neighbouring gun
Bird may fly or beast may run,
let this maxim e'er be thine:
Follow not across the line.
Stops and beaters oft unseen
lurk behind some leafy screen;
calm and steady always be:
never shoot where you can't see.
You may kill or you may miss,
but at all times think of this:
All the pheasants ever bred
won't repay for one man dead.

(Written in 1909 by Mark Beaufoy, M.P., for his son, Henry M. Beaufoy, on reaching the age of 13.)

A MOTHER'S ADVICE TO HER DAUGHTER

So, my darling daughter, you have been invited to a shoot.

Let us suppose that this is the first time such an invitation has been made to you and, most correctly, you have come to seek your mother's guidance on the matter; much has been written on this subject for the edification of young gentlemen but not, as far as I am aware, for those of the fairer sex. The reason for this is simple: you must remember that, as far as shooting is concerned, you will be regarded by every male as a member of not the fairer, but the inferior, sex.

By and large in this country ladies do not shoot. A lady is asked to join a shooting party in order to provide light and merry conversation in the shooting brake between drives; to hand round mugs of soup if so required at luncheon; to carry (should there be no loaders) a cartridge bag and, most important of all, to provide moral support for whichever gentleman kindly allows her to stand behind him during the drive.

She should in fact be like the best sort of gun-dog: attractive but not flashy; silent, competent and biddable.

You may be asked to stand with a gentleman during one of the drives; you may even ask for the privilege yourself with the words 'Would you mind?' or 'Would it bother you if I stood with you during the next drive?' This, however, will not be a popular suggestion either with very young gentlemen, who may be nervous about their shooting ability, or with the wives of older gentlemen who may be nervous about their husbands' ability to concentrate solely on the birds of the air.

At any rate if you are permitted to stand behind a gun, you are not there just for the sake of your blue eyes. You have a duty to perform.

You must not speak until spoken to. You may, if the task has been required of you, murmur 'to your right', or 'to your left', if you think that the gentleman has possibly failed to notice the approach of a bird from that quarter. On no account must you lose your self-control or raise your voice, or be heard calling enthusiastically 'Here, up there, now there's another one, quick, didn't you see it? It was right over your head . . .'

This would be considered not only a Hindrance, but an Outrage.

You should watch carefully where each bird falls. Runners should not be announced to the world at large by remarks such as 'Ah, poor thing, it's gone hobbling off under that bush' but should be marked, silently, for picking up later. Above all you should never comment upon the performance of other guns but concentrate solely upon Him whose companion you are for that drive as you will be expected later to discuss, knowledgeably and accurately (should he introduce the subject) every shot the gentleman has taken, and praise him intelligently on his prowess.

If by some inexplicable chance he has missed a bird (usually referred to as 'the one which eluded me') there are various phrases which you may use to assuage his ruffled pride: 'on the curl' or 'it was going at the most extraordinary angle' or, best of all, 'how right you were to leave it'.

Where you actually stand in relation to the gentleman is of prime importance. Stand far enough back that you are not nudging his elbow and yet not so far that, when he turns to fire at a bird going away behind, he will find your charming face looking down his barrels. It is also useful to remember that an English lady is often moderately tall and therefore, when standing behind a gentleman who is even an inch or so shorter, it is imperative to watch for the first hint of his turning round and to duck (discreetly) at the appropriate moment. No gentleman would wish to be seen striking a lady over the head with his gun: it would do untold damage to the barrels.

In the absence of his own loader, the gentleman may ask you to load for him. This is a service which on no account should you ever volunteer to undertake of your own accord: it plays havoc with nerves, nails and ears and almost invariably calls upon you a great deal of abuse. Nevertheless, should the task be required of you, however glacial the temperature of the day REMOVE YOUR GLOVES. The gentleman will not take kindly to bits of woollen thumb in his breech. The damage to your hand or glove will be a matter of indifference to him: what does matter is that he will be unable to close his gun. He will miss the shot, and you will be cursed.

CLOTHING

Speaking of gloves, let us review the matter of clothing. As previously mentioned you should look attractive, but definitely not glamorous. 'Glamour' is not a word to be found in English shooting parlance; 'well turned out' or 'looks well'—or the supreme compliment of 'a very fetching rig'—but never glamorous.

Waiting for hours during a winter shoot you will want to be—and must be, for gentlemen have no time for ladies who whinge about the weather —comfortable and above all warm.

If you must wear a scarf, it should be woollen—a silk scarf when rained upon affords its owner the appearance of a waterlogged spaniel. If there be amongst the company some young man with whom you are in love, you may wear his hat.

A shooting stick is perfectly acceptable, but never one of those cumbersome tripod chairs now so favoured by elderly Continental shots. A bag may be taken, provided that it be of the shoulder-bag variety and not carried in the hand, and should be of the type very nearly indistinguishable from a cartridge bag; in this you may carry a hip-flask. Malt whisky or cherry brandy is considered satisfactory provided that you do not drink it yourself during drives.

Unlike the gentleman who only wears leather on his feet a lady may—and in winter should—wear green rubber boots for winter shooting; leather boots will not do and in any case are most uncomfortable if the ground is clay based, when you emerge at the end of a long wet drive looking like a carthorse with great unshakeable mounds of earth on your feet.

For summer shooting, you will of course, emulate the gentleman, and wear leather shoes, brown and laced and preferably with those nice fringed leather flaps which cover the laces and ensure they do not get caught up in the heather.

Clothes should obviously be discreet in colour: greens, browns and in autumn rust-colour—in the South—whilst grey-blue tweeds, or green and heather colours, are perfectly correct for a day in the North. Unless you are known as a shot yourself, breeches could look wrong; and if you are a shot, you will know well enough to eschew any other than those made of loden cloth, moleskin or the tweed variety that may be purchased from those very fine gunsmiths in the West End of London. Especially to be avoided are velvet corduroy breeches, which are fit only for sitting in by the fire: they look as unprofessional as they are, shrinking rapidly and visibly at the first drop of rain, and being remarkably magnetic to dog hairs. A pair of well-cut trousers, or a divided skirt of fine tweed, worn with an open-necked shirt in summer and a coat of the Barbour variety in winter, is correct; suits, or matching skirt and jackets, look 'town' and therefore Unprofessional—a word which is to be found frequently in the English shooting vocabulary.

With the changing times loden capes are now in order, but should have horn, not silver, buttons. They should always be discarded, however, if you are asked to load, even in a downpour. Without proper sleeves they do tend to get in the way of the business in hand. On really cold days fur is acceptable but only if worn as a lining to your coat.

A racoon hat is permissible if you are known to your hostess, as is also a muff provided that it be quite obviously a shooting muff of leather or canvas and lined in beaver or sheepskin. Any other fur smacks of the townee or worse; the offending object will be the subject of much derision and will be thrown in the back of a Land Rover where it will be trampled by the beaters and savaged by the dogs.

Gloves should be woollen; if you have to pick up at the end of a drive you will find that feathers do not stick as closely to wool as they do to leather and, should you retrieve a pheasant that has been shot in the head, though it will come down quite dead it will bleed profusely, and blood will ruin a skin glove. And you will remember, too late, that it is never correct to carry a dead bird by its feet ...

LADIES AS SHOTS

Although it is an accepted fact that Continental women shoot (you will scarcely go out for a day abroad without seeing at least one female bearing a gun, and making a good show of it too) the intelligence that a lady shoots is greeted, in this country, with the same sort of reaction that would result from an announcement of impending war: disbelief, coupled with horrified dismay.

English ladies, given the fact that they are allowed to exist at all in the shooting field, are not supposed to shoot. The role of the female is as strictly defined as the role of the gun-dog and both, as far as a gentleman is concerned, should remain strictly to heel.

Lady shots, in so far as they are admitted any existence at all, are considered in the same light as female drivers—a breed to be skirted warily at worst, and avoided at best.

In a sense there is good reason for this: as ladies are not supposed to shoot, ladies in general do not do so. Not only because for a very long time (and in spite of splendid Edwardian photographs of ladies in large hats and bustled skirts pretending to cope with high pheasants) it was considered to be an Un-Ladylike pastime, and therefore any of the distaff side bearing a gun might be regarded as tough, tomboyish and un-feminine (in 1882 Queen Victoria herself had written in a letter to her daughter, that although it was perfectly acceptable for a woman to be a spectator, only 'fast women' shot); not only because of that but because, since ladies supposedly 'do not shoot', they are never invited to do so.

Now it is a well-known fact that you can only become proficient in anything at all by a great deal of practice at it. So it is with shooting: in order to shoot well you must shoot often. No lady, however, is *ever* asked to shoot unless it be a known and corroborated fact that she shoots WELL, and this of course can only be achieved if she shoots frequently; but no host will ask a lady to shoot unless he has it on unimpeachable authority that not only can she shoot straight but that she is also a safe shot. No sensible host will ask an 'unknown quantity' (unless it be his bank manager, a species even in these modern times almost exclusively male) and risk upsetting his friends and annoying his keepers.

So where is a lady shot to begin?

26

If it be your good fortune to be allied, by inheritance or marriage, to a property which provides a shoot, your first hurdle is easily overcome. For on your own shoot you may do as you wish, and miss as many birds as you may, and it will all be taken in good part PROVIDED ONLY that you never pretend to be anything more than a complete novice in the art of holding a gun straight. But being a novice does not mean being a fool or a liability; and if it is immediately apparent to your cautious or perhaps appalled gentlemen friends that you are, if not a fine shot nor yet even a moderately competent shot, but at least a perfectly SAFE shot, then the second hurdle is conquered. A lady, however straight she shoots, however many lessons she has taken, however many hours she has spent waiting at the end of the line praying for just one, please God, bird to come down, must always be—AND BE SEEN TO BE—safe. So to be over-cautious is a failing which can earn you nothing but respect from the gentlemen who stand next to you, to say nothing of the beaters and the pickers-up.

So let us assume that you are now a Lady Shot. That you have spent the first requisite number of years braving cold, rain or midges for an evening pigeon to come in; tramping alone hoping for a chance at a rabbit or a snipe or even a woodcock; walking hedgerows for the odd pheasant; that you have then spent the next requisite number of seasons at the end of the line on your own shoot where the beaters will cheer encouragement and the rest of the guns will watch to see what you can do; and then (all this, mind you, takes far less time for a gentleman to achieve)—then, when you can stand in line and manage to bring down, safely and cleanly, enough birds to feel that you have done your duty, you might hear the magic words 'not a bad shot, that girl'—SPOKEN BY A GENTLEMAN— then, you have truly begun.

But it is not enough for a lady to be considered 'not a bad shot'. A lady, if she is to shoot in the company of gentlemen who may be—it is not unknown—perfectly rotten shots themselves, should be a Good Shot. She should of course never be so good as to embarrass the gentlemen for whom, let it never be forgotten, the sport is arranged. There are only a handful of ladies in every generation who are Good, and very few indeed who are Very Good. And the magic moment when you discover that you have arrived at this stage will be when you overhear the words—again spoken by a gentleman TO ANOTHER GENTLEMAN—'a damn fine shot'. No use of the word 'she' or 'that girl', you will notice. No mention of gender. In short, asexual.

And it is then you will know that you have, at last, been accepted as an equal in the shooting field.

Having been awarded this crown of equality, of asexual equality, by your peers (who will, however well you shoot, always remain your superiors) now and only now is the time to remind them that you are after all a lady. For the past years you have striven to banish any such thought from their minds: you have trudged the fields in old clothes and smelly mackintoshes looking like the wrath of God; you have belaboured your dog when it failed to meet demands, caught your own runners unseen, raged alone against your incompetencies.

Alone, you may still do so; in public, never; and all the criteria which are applicable to the gentleman shot must be assumed by you to an even higher degree.

Your turnout, like your manners, will be impeccable, your modesty charming and your femininity unquestioned. This is not to say that you will not have to climb fences, cross ditches unaided, pick up your own game, get bruised, wet and sworn at and suffer every ignominy of fate—for you will.

But because you are a Lady, not merely a hoyden with a gun, the gentlemen will appreciate all the more the fact that you love what is, after all, their sport; and that you have striven to make your participation in it so easy, and so pleasant, for them to accept.

OUT AND ABOUT

Some hosts do not admit the presence of the fairer sex under any circumstances whatever in the shooting field which, like the dining-room table when the port is circulated, they deem fit for men alone. I have attended numerous shoots—albeit in East Anglia and hosted by rather elderly gentlemen—where the women and the drinks were only allowed out at lunch and then sent home afterwards.

A lady, therefore, when asked to attend a shooting party, must come prepared for the fact that her presence in the field may be—depending on the idiosyncrasies of her host—of minimal duration, and that the rest of the day may well be spent indoors in the company of her hostess and the other females of the party doing the flowers, making herself charming to the cook, taking the aged pug for a walk, leafing through the glossy magazines or writing letters on the crested paper provided in her bedroom.

A lady is therefore advised to arrive for a weekend shooting party prepared for all contingencies and to include in her luggage both a small address book and a piece of interesting *petit point*. This is especially important when accepting invitations abroad where the reading matter available may not be at all what the lady is used to.

Should you be invited to a shooting party abroad it is worth noting that the customs regarding ladies in the shooting field differ enormously from country to country, as is only to be expected.

Some countries are quite like England in some respects, others not at all, and so you should be aware of any pitfalls or hazards since your Continental host may well encourage, or condone, behaviour or appearance or manners which might appear to you totally alien from those required by the English gentlemen with whom you usually find yourself in the shooting field.

CHAPEAUX
HOLLANDAIS

Holland, for instance, is most nearly akin to East Anglia in matters concerning the presence of females in the shooting field. That is to say as a lady, you will not be expected to stay out for the whole day.

On the other hand if you look at a group of Dutch women on a shoot, it is perhaps understandable why Dutch men prefer them to stay at home.

39

Dutch women on Dutch shoots all wear that type of loden cloth peculiar to Holland which is of a singular shade of green well known by any dog owner whose hound has just eaten a surfeit of young grass. All Dutch women wear hats with shaving brushes on the side, and brooches in the shape of oak leaves into which are set the tusks, or wisdom teeth, or large stags shot by their husbands. Husbands are the only men behind whom Dutch women are allowed to stand. Dutch women do not speak, sit or smoke during drives or indeed at any other time, and silently hand round plates of complicated little things at lunch before the regulation speeches from the guest of honour, the foreign guest and the 'high gun' of the morning.

They do not, you are inclined to feel, have a very jolly life.

A-BROAD IN
BELGIUM

Belgian women out shooting do, however, have a very jolly life indeed. Belgian women sit behind their lovers not their husbands during drives. All Belgian women overdress: full make-up, unisex scent, a furrier's ransom of skins and suedes and heavy gold jewellery, together with silk scarves (if it rains Belgian women stay in Range Rovers) and delightfully coloured turbans make Belgian women a delight to the eye and a menace to the lovers behind whom they sit on tripod stools.

I was once present at a shoot in Belgium during which one woman, dressed in a rust-coloured suede trouser suit and a large red fur hat, narrowly escaped extinction at the hands of an Italian who fired—having mistaken her for a fox—when she went to look for a suitable bush for privacy in the middle of a drive.

MORAL (1)

Although gentlemen may 'disappear' quite respectably, when out in the shooting field a lady is expected to be like unto the angels in every respect, and to be deaf to every call other than that of 'MARK THAT BIRD!'

'TRÈS CHIC, TRÈS SNOB, PRESQUE CAD'

(Sign seen in a man's shop in Paris)

French women, when out shooting either in France or in this country, wear 'un petit tweed anglais' of beautiful and subtle colouring that speaks volumes for the Faubourg Saint-Honoré and nothing at all for the Isle of Harris. The tweed is invariably made into a suit, edged with leather, by the best English gentleman's tailor. French women also wear deerstalkers' hats with the bows tied small, proper shooting brogues, lacy stockings and, in cold weather, prettily coloured Shetland shooting stockings held in place by braid garters with little v's cut into the ends. (English gentlemen also need to

hold up their shooting stockings by
some sort of garter, but usually use an
old bit of what is known as 'Four b'
Two'.)

French women have cartridge-
sized atomisers of Joy which fit into
little inner pockets of monogrammed
shoulder bags, and use gold lighters
covered in brown crocodile skin. They
do not load, and never pick up.

STARS AND STRIPES

American women (though scarcely, if ever, asked to attend a shoot in this country—a fact which also applies to most American men) usually wear bright red or white somewhere about the upper half of their anatomy. This is why you will rarely see an American woman being encouraged to sit with anyone except her husband if he is shooting, and exhorted to 'have a lovely lie in, darling, these silly drives are so boring' if he is not.

American women often get kitted up at the Scotch House before venturing out into the shooting world, which makes them easy targets for ribaldry especially amongst Scottish keepers. They don't wear scent because they have been told not to, but do wear large gold bracelets clanging with large gold coins because they haven't.

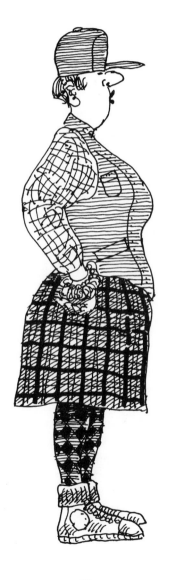

VIVA ESPAÑA

Spanish women all look like 'rejonea-doras'—leather riding chaps, masses of suede fringes and manes of streaked blonde hair. They also wear wide-brimmed black hats, leather shooting boots with zips up the inside of the leg from Diana's in Madrid, and elaborate bullfighters' shirts made to measure in Seville. Silver buttons, dark nail varnish and black Sobranie cigarettes which are kept in a small tasselled pouch attached to the belt (also from Diana's) complete the ensemble.

A Spanish woman talks all the time during drives, sits on a three-legged stool and kicks the dead birds to prove she's man enough. She will also clap enthusiastically over any shot she has happened to notice, and shouts encouragement to friends down the line.

FRØM THE
FRØZEN NØRTH

Scandinavian women are almost invariably blonde—not a good shooting
colour—and wear fur hats with ear
pieces tied on top by means of little
leather thongs. When these are let
down to combat Arctic weather, the
wearer is cut off from most forms of
communication with the outside
world which with certain Scandinavian women is just as well. During the
'hunting season' in their own country,
houses are by tradition lit mostly by
candles, resulting in jocular com-
ments the following morning about
bloodshot eyes.

If a Scandinavian woman turns up
for a shoot in this country with bloodshot eyes, it is not up to the English
lady to make remarks—however
justified—about them.

53

VOLARE

Italian women (and Italian men come to that) are not in the least interested in the Art of Shooting, but they do like to shoot. Italian men also like picking up after the drive if there are any English ladies to help. If not, not.

Never volunteer to sit behind an Italian man during a drive. In the first place, you will be deafened, as all Italians have their cartridges especially built for them with the maximum load, to enable them to hit things out of range to an English gentleman; in the second place if there is an Italian wife, she will be so incensed at your setting your cap at her husband in thus brazen a fashion (for they do not understand the ritual of the thing at all) that she will vociferate abuse at, or about, you throughout the drive from as much as three or four places away down the line, and will later manage to trip up with a glass of cherry brandy when you are conveniently to hand.

54

BY THE
WAY . . .

Cherry brandy is extremely difficult to remove from any form of clothing.

A small handbag-sized atomiser of cleaning fluid may be carefully kept in your handbag in case of emergencies—to be used discreetly and in private.

ACHTUNG

German women out shooting are almost always plain, and almost always widows. This is quite simply explained by the fact that in Germany, instead of standing waiting for nice high birds to be driven over the line as usually happens elsewhere, it is deemed more exciting for the guns to face each other from either end of, say, a belt of corn or barley and then to advance slowly towards each other, firing when anything appears. (This is the famous Blücher manoeuvre, of 'line faces line'.)

Now whilst in this country the success of a shoot is measured not only by the size of the bag but also by the 'quality' of the birds—the higher and more difficult the better—the Germans have not yet learned to differentiate between quality and quantity. It therefore follows that any bird, however low to the ground, is considered fair game in order to increase the bag—'if it moves, shoot it'—and so when a bird so much as shows itself out of the barley both lines of guns open fire, *towards each other* and at head height.

MORAL (2)

When you go shooting in Germany, it is imperative therefore to wear comfortable loose-fitting clothes in which you may flatten yourself to the ground at a moment's notice, as the bag at the end of a day's shoot usually includes one fatality, a number of walking wounded, and a huge quantity of birds which, due to the fact that they have been blasted at from extremely close range, give the appearance of being plucked, gutted and oven-ready.

You do not, under any circumstances, pick up anything in Germany.

ACHTUNG (CONT.): THE BUSINESS SHOOT

You will on occasion be asked to attend The Business Shoot in Germany. This is an immensely organised, almost totally male, affair involving a lot of schnapps and large men in loud checks (the latter jovially referred to as 'ze English tveed ja?') who are driven to their stands in stretch-model Mercedes cars, accompanied by huge silent gorillas whom, although they are referred to as loaders, everybody knows to be bodyguards.

The women and the widows do not appear until lunch when they emerge like lemmings from the back of the Mercedes cars in which they have crouched, terrorised by the body-guards, during the morning, and into which they are again despatched for the afternoon. As this ensures that they are the only form of life not to be shot at during the proceedings, it is probably a Good Thing.

At the end of the day the game is laid out in neat and interminable lines of which Blücher would have no doubt approved, with torches at each of the four corners, and the hunting horns are then sounded—a different call for each type of game shot. It is picturesque and romantic, and unquestionably the best part of the day.

LAST WORD

The important thing for an English lady to remember when attending a shoot on the Continent is that, as I have said previously, customs and manners vary enormously according to each country. The only thing that is required of you therefore is that you should watch, and assimilate, and enthuse gracefully however strange it may all appear.

Never complain, and never compare, and keep your eyes peeled.

If all else fails, you can always close them (at the end of the day) and think of England.

A LADY IS INVITED TO GO STALKING

You have been asked to go stalking in Scotland; not to shoot, as of course ladies do not shoot, but to follow behind for a day on the hill, to watch, to participate in and enjoy what is undoubtedly one of the finest of sports in the wild and remote and possibly most beautiful parts of our kingdom.

Now, contrary to all the myths surrounding it, stalking is not chic. It may be chic to be ASKED to go stalking, it may be chic to have BEEN stalking; but as to the actual stalk itself, that may be a myriad of things—exhilarating, tortuous, incredible, back-breaking, exhausting, heart-pounding, magical and the most memorable day of your life; but it is definitely not 'chic'.

The reason for this lies quite simply in the fact that you have been asked 'for a day's stalking'. And that is exactly what it is: a whole day out, on the hills. It may swelter or pour, there may be hail or a heatwave, you may be more tired than you thought possible and ache in places you never dreamed existed but, once you have set off behind the stalker, there is no turning back.

No nipping into the Land Rover to shelter from the rain; no quiet moments sitting on a shooting stick admiring the view; no relaxing by the fire over lunch; no light and cheerful banter; you just walk.

And it is not just walking, either; you will climb and crawl, scramble over rocks, slither through streams, hang over waterfalls, clutch onto heather; wait silent for hours, aching with cold or eaten by midges; crouch against snow, battle against horizontal rain, climb until you think you will burst, and then climb again.

And short of breaking a leg and being carried down the hill by an unspeaking stalker or your seething host, there is nothing you can do except to plough on uncomplaining, alert, biddable ... your only comfort that of knowing that, rather like banging your head against a wall, it will be wonderful when you stop.

That is not the worst part of the day.

The worst part is right at the beginning standing at the bottom of the hill, with the stalker checking the rifle and making dour and incomprehensible noises about what he thinks of the weather, and your host being jolly and cheerful and strapping on luncheon-bags and telescopes and checking the flares and the blade of his knife and the knots on his laces and looking up into the sky and saying things like 'They'll be high up today, eh Donald? No messing about, we'll just go straight up to the tops don't you think?' and you lift your gaze unto the mountains from whence cometh no help at all and know, KNOW, that you were totally wrong to accept this chic invitation to 'come and stalk'.

The first time that I was asked to go stalking was one sodden and miserable October. I fell out of the overnight train in my London clothes and into a thunderstorm to be met by a keeper wearing tweeds so hirsute they must have required mowing at night. We drove for an hour, deafened in the Land Rover, up the glen to his cottage where my host would be waiting and I would change.

My host, correctly turned out in a shabby tweed suit, cap, climbing boots and a thumb-stick, was chatting amicably to the keeper's wife as we drew up, both of them apparently unaware that the heavens had opened and Niagara was coming down over the porch. The keeper carried my suitcase into the bathroom which I found I was sharing with a duck who apparently always lived under the basin.

I opened my case: there were the two long dresses for that evening (always two, in case something happens), the clothes for the smart lunch the next day, more clothes for the relaxed and cosy evening to follow, skirts and blouses, sweaters and scarves; silk pochettes for underwear (in case the butler unpacked) and the lacy négligé (in case the housekeeper laid out one's things at night); the *petit point* and the address book; the clothes for stalking. And no trousers.

Not a pair of breeches, not a pair of jeans—nothing. I had all the things I'd read you were supposed to have: the boots, the thick socks, the green textured tights; the camouflage Barbour (a masterstroke I thought) and the woollen scarf; the regulation two handkerchiefs, one green large for blowing into, one white large for getting lost with; the piece of string, the anti-midge gel, the safety-pin IN CASE, the pocket knife. I'd done my homework, I'd learned all about what you were supposed to do out stalking, I knew you had to walk in single file and not utter, I'd done skiing exercises to get fit, I'd brought everything there was to bring and I'd forgotten to pack the trousers.

The rain was lashing at the window, the entire contents of the suitcase were by this time all over the floor, the duck didn't like it much, I was beginning to panic and wonder what a lady should do under the circumstances when there was a knock at the door.

'The laird was wondering if you'd care to take Donald's waterproofs, miss' came the voice of the keeper's wife. 'It's terrible wet out and they're a puckle torn but that way you'll keep your knees a wee bitty dry.'

So it was that I emerged for my novice's day on the hill perfectly turned out from the waist up, and wearing my textured green tights under the keeper's old mackintosh trousers with the string round the tops and the In Case safety-pin holding the fly fronts together.

The bath that night was the deepest, the darkest brown peatiest, and the best I had ever had; and nobody ever knew.

LADIES AS
RIFLE SHOTS

If it is considered 'un-ladylike' to shoot
with a gun, to shoot with a rifle is (to
the world in general and to gentlemen
in particular) doubly so. The very
posture you are required to assume is
not one in which the feminine form
may be seen to its best advantage—
sprawled out shooting on the ground
in the classic 'prone military position'
does absolutely nothing for a lady's
sense of the elegant; and whereas you
can wear clothes which do you justice
when shooting with a gun, there is
nothing to recommend stalking clothes
to any lady seeking to look her best.

This, however, is immaterial. As we
have previously mentioned you must
look businesslike and CORRECTLY
turned out for the occasion (which is
after all the criterion of dressing for
any event) and if, to be accepted as a
rifle shot, a lady has to appear looking

like something out of a war department surplus store in order to blend in with the hill, it matters not one jot.

To become a good rifle shot takes a lady very much less time than to become a good shot with a gun; shooting with a gun requires, as we have seen, years of patience, effort and practice and, to be able to continue shooting well, you must continue shooting regularly.

With a rifle, however, once you have learned to hold the rifle correctly, keep a steady aim, squeeeeeeze the trigger and fire, no amount of practice at paper targets will make you any better a *shot*. You can practise taking different *types* of shot—lying down, sitting or standing—all of which do require perseverance, but basically you either can or you cannot—you either 'have an eye' for it or you have not. If you have not, then your stalking will be as a spectator and none the less enjoyable for that; if you do 'have an eye' for it, and your stalk culminates in shooting the given beast cleanly and well, to the total satisfaction of the stalker and of yourself, then you are lucky, and very privileged.

This is precisely why ladies are neither assumed to be good rifle shots nor often encouraged to become so: no man can accept that someone other than of his own sex could have the ability to shoot a rifle straight.

Rifles are, after all, weapons eminently masculine in concept: they were weapons of war, which was a masculine duty; they were built by men, carried by men, named after men: Martini Henry, Mauser, Winchester, vom Hofe, Mannlicher, Rigby; reference is made to the muzzle-loader, the breech-loader, the heavy bolt action; there are rifles which are said to 'have a kick like a mule'. A man is surely required to cope with all this.

There is nothing, however, to preclude a lady from trying . . .

There is also nothing to preclude a lady from being as good a shot as, or possibly even a better shot than, the gentlemen who view this contingency with such disbelief: it is not a question of gender, merely of ability coupled with a large amount of luck.

Of course there is more to stalking than the ability to hit the bull's-eye, as many a perfectly competent gentleman rifle shot has found to his cost. Stalking also entails the stalk; and the ability to fire a steady shot having just grappled your way up the final hundred yards, clinging to an outcrop by your toes in the teeth of a howling gale and with your heart beating in your ears, requires stamina, courage and good nerves—and luck.

UP THE HILL

However good a rifle shot you may have proved yourself to be, however kindly the gods may look upon your efforts, your day's stalking could not even begin to take place without one vital element: the stalker.

The stalker belongs to a unique and usually eccentric breed: fiercely possessive of his terrain he knows every beast and bird on it; his duties include that of a keeper but he is also guide, mentor, companion and confidant. He thinks like a poacher and acts like God. His word is law and everything—your fate, your reputation, your packed lunch—is in his hands.

If he likes you, you will—all things being equal—be presented with a shootable stag. If he does not, nothing will be said but you will find yourself being taken, as by some latter-day old Duke of York, for a very long route-march up and down the hills.

It is worth remembering at this point that, although they are always referred to as 'hills', the greater part of stalking takes place in what may well number amongst the highest mountains in the country.

At the onset, the stalker will regard any lady whom he is bidden to take out on the hill with the gravest misgivings even though, gentleman that he is, he may not give full vent to those misgivings in your presence. The long silences, however, and the baleful glare as you bid him good-morning will leave you in no doubt as to the enthusiasm with which he anticipates a day out alone with this latest guest.

He will have cast a discerning eye over your clothing, silently registering the fact that you look correct and comfortable, and that you have obviously taken the precaution of ascertaining what 'colour' hill you are about to embark on. (This is vital: to turn up for a day's stalking on a 'yellow' hill such as you will find, say, in Glen Lyon during September, when all the ferns are golden, wearing a dark green tweed would be unforgivable and would entail the wrath of God and your being despatched back to change. Stalkers are tyrants.)

He will then have watched you fire your regulation three practice shots at the iron target and, if you are lucky, will be heard to mutter something like 'Well, that'll just have to do' in tones of the deepest gloom. You both then climb into his vehicle and set off, a ruse designed solely in order to give him the opportunity of finding out as much as possible about you, your stalking experience and your genealogy in the shortest possible time with the least possible conversational charm. 'You'll not have stalked before, I daresay' is the usual opening gambit.

At this juncture, a lady would be well advised to be as wary as possible. If you are a novice, admit it at once but if you have had any experience of stalking at all, keep silent: the stalker will find out soon enough in any case but, if there is one thing that he dislikes more than taking a lady out on the hill (you may possibly have heard him mutter 'och, a b . . . . . WUMMan' as he met you in the morning), it is taking a lady out *who is reputed to shoot well*. This offends his sense of propriety, his pride, and his ancestors.

Your day will be a misery: he will set off at a smart pace and never look back; he will pause to spy through his glass only long enough for you to catch up with him whereupon, as you fall thankfully into a heap at his feet with a totally new meaning of the line 'as pants the hart' ringing in your ears, he will growl 'We've stopped long enough, the beasts'll nae wait for us' and set off again with a light springing step over the heather; he will take the longest way round, bark instructions into the wind and finally present you with an absolutely impossible shot (the back of a stag's head showing behind a rock, say, at 250 yards) with the triumphant words 'There ye'are then' flung like a gauntlet.

And when you have failed to let the rifle off (since the beast has obviously heard the challenge too and, without pausing to give you even the chance of a shot, has taken off like a lamplighter into the distant yonder) and you are turning round to mumble apologies for your clumsiness, you will just be able to perceive a hunched and furious figure stomping away from you, 50 yards downhill, head held low and wearing a black cloud.

You unload the rifle and scrabble to your feet, collecting sight covers, rifle cover, binoculars, knapsack and stick and, trying to make sense of the seemingly endless yards of straps and webbings, set off at an ungainly gallop to catch him up. 'Well, that's that then' comes the snarl; and you know you are on your way home.

But not every stalk is a disaster. If the lady is quiet (stalkers hate women who 'chirrup') and well-mannered, modest and charming, not over-confident and yet clearly at ease, he will regard her as, possibly, a moderate sort of day's work. And then, if she manages to shoot cleanly whatever is presented to her, or apologises immediately and never makes excuses for herself if she fails, and is helpful and good-humoured and appreciative of all his effort, then he will be content.

And when your stalker is content, your cup is full . . .

Whether or not the elements have been kind, whether you have shot the trophy head of a lifetime or some poor-conditioned and miserable 'switch' —whether or not indeed you have fired the rifle at all—matters not one scrap. You will have enjoyed a day up the hill. You may have lain peacefully for hours watching a herd of red deer, rust against the ferns, or the shadow of an eagle soaring over a scree; heard an old cock grouse ticking away in the heather; picked blueberries, drunk the sweetest of waters trickling between mosses, watched the ravens tumbling and playing high above; perhaps you stalked down by the sea-shore where the otters are, and where the seals lie stretched out in the sun; or, later in the year crunched through the snow and heard the ptarmigan whirring away over the rocks.

You will have shared your lunch and talked and talked—stories, tales, yarns, cabbages and kings—your only sense of time the lengthening shadows or, later, a sliver of a moon.

And then for home.

All the horrors—the climbing, the agonies of nerves, the midges or the cold—are forgotten. Your boots no longer hurt, the rifle is as light as a feather, the long walk back a pleasure to be savoured with a fine companion. Tired and contented, you share a thermos of sweet tea before climbing back into the van—a job well done and the time too fast gone.

'A fine day, wifey'; and you will know that you have earned yourself a true friend.

DIANA THE HUNTRESS

In earlier days the lawful season for venery, which began on Midsummer's Day and lasted until Holy Rood Day, used to be called 'the Time of Grace'.

The ancient art of venery—the taking of red deer and roe deer by stealth—exists in many other parts of the world such as the Americas, Europe or India. Elsewhere too big game is stalked; but game in general is hunted in many different fashions according to differing countries and differing traditions.

The nobly-born patron of stag hunting became Bishop of Liège in the seventh century, and the Feast of Saint Hubert is now a national day on the Continent: but the Romans chose a goddess to preside over the chase, thus ensuring that the fairer sex might indeed grace the sport.

A lady should be aware of what may be expected of her at all times and in every circumstance; this is especially important if you are asked to shoot game abroad where the old adage of 'When in Rome...' is particularly appropriate.

You may be asked to shoot stags in Spain, for instance; here you will partake in a 'monteria' which entails riding up into the mountains, setting up camp in an appointed place amongst the rocks, lighting a fire and taking something good to read. You will wait here during the whole day, and will remember that the description once given of war—long periods of intense boredom punctuated by short periods of intense activity—can be applied to other situations as you wait for a fleeting chance at a beast hurtling past you, the noise of pursuing dogs far behind, and then silence again.

In the Ardennes, however, you stand behind a tree while packs of assorted hounds rush yelping through the tall misty forests and whatever exists in the form of wild life—roe deer, red deer, boar, magpies and the odd wild-cat—pours out across the rides between the 'guns'. A dozen or so rifles crack as one and you recollect the fact that Waterloo is not so far away and that it was a 'damned close-run thing' even then.

Elsewhere on the Continent, you may be asked to shoot from a high seat.

You get up just before dawn and, having walked or climbed for miles, you then clamber up onto a sort of palisaded platform in a tree from where, freezing and damp, you watch the sun coming up, the steam rising from your sodden clothes, the midges gathering playfully around you and the game wandering out to feed below.

As well as midges, gnats and various interesting forms of insect life you will also have for company a very smart and loden-caped keeper with you (whose dog is patiently sitting under the high seat, waiting for something to happen) so you may not take anything to read.

You may also be asked to go and shoot moose in Norway. I would strongly advise against it.

Here you set off well before dawn with a keeper, a husky dog and your host who, in case you miss your shot, is also carrying a rifle. (They think of everything in Norway.) The dog is unleashed and disappears into the mountains. Perhaps an hour later you hear barking which means that it has caught up with, and is now you hope following, a moose, so you all take off in hot pursuit. These words are not to be taken lightly: through the forest you go, through the knee-deep snow, through valley and gorges, torrents and passes—all day, *at a run*. You return on your knees at dark, are bidden to remove all your clothes, are left for dead in a sauna and then whipped with birch twigs and put out into the snow. This is apparently the only way in Norway of avoiding rigor mortis.

Go to Mongolia and shoot sheep, go to Alaska for bear or Corsica where the mouflons are, go to Austria to chase chamois dancing on pinnacles above the snow-line . . . But not moose.

'IF A SPORTS-
MAN TRUE
YOU'D BE'

It must of course be accepted without
question, as has been said previously
many times, that shooting whether it
be with a gun or with a rifle is considered by most people in general, and
by all gentlemen in particular, to be a
purely masculine pastime and a
purely masculine achievement. 'I have
met ladies who shoot', the Earl of
Warwick was reputed to have said,
'and I have come to the conclusion,
being no longer young and a staunch
Conservative, that I would prefer them
not to.' So be it.

If however you as a lady *are* permitted to share their sport and can do so with tact and charm, never as a competitor (a most un-ladylike trait) but always as an appreciative participator, then you will have done well; if you can also assuage their doubts and set their hearts at ease, then you will have done very well.

The accolade of 'sportsman' is, in the end, one of approval for, and of pleasure in, a kindred spirit who will share and understand a sport as well as having respect, and love, for it. The word does not denote a gender but a quality and, as with all things worth while, it is hard-earned.

This proves one thing more, namely that you must never take anything for granted. As Cromwell was reputed to have said to his soldiers: 'Put your trust in God, but keep your powder dry.'

I can think of no finer advice for any lady.